Tips for a Fantastic Wedding

When You Have Just a Little Time and Money

Dana World Patterson

authorHOUSE®

AuthorHouse™
1663 Liberty Drive
Bloomington, IN 47403
www.authorhouse.com
Phone: 1-800-839-8640

First published by AuthorHouse 1/14/2010

ISBN: 978-1-4389-0194-7 (sc)

Library of Congress Control Number: 2009912741

Printed in the United States of America
Bloomington, Indiana

This book is printed on acid-free paper.

For my guys,
Giles, Caleb and Jordan

You're the best!

Psalms 37:23

Contents

Preface

In 1996, my husband and I planned our wedding in 30 days. Since then we have helped countless couples have a beautiful wedding, albeit budget-wise weddings within various timeframes. Our No. 1 priority is to help couples see the bigger picture is beyond the wedding day. A "BIG MARRIAGE" is of parallel concern and not loosing focus of a big marriage while planning your wedding can be accomplished.

You may want a wedding with all the trimmings, but there is no way your budget can accommodate your dream. I understand that. My husband and I pooled our resources, sold a few items and used the money that we had on hand to create an elegant wedding. So, before you consider a "Las Vegas quickie" or a trip to the Courthouse, sit down and prioritize. Speak with one another, your parents, or anyone financially responsible for the wedding about expectations and desires. That means really thinking about what is important to you, what can be modified or what you can live without.

Remember that first impressions count. One grand gesture immediately sets the tone and mood for your wedding from beginning to end. Think big, but remain realistic and true to your budget to create an atmosphere that no one will forget and you will enjoy.

Make separate lists of your likes and dislikes, such as, food, color preferences, music, and your ideal atmosphere. These factors will assist in planning your special day. With a limited timeframe and money, this book will be your guide and provide 14 simple tips for a beautiful and affordable wedding. Write in it and use it as a resource book.

Remember, time will move swiftly. Stay focused on your fiancé, priorities, and your budget. You may want a "big wedding", however, your ultimate goal should always be a "Big Marriage". A marriage that is solid and lifelong.

Tip #1
Getting Started

Tip #1   Getting Started

- ♥ Soon you will be married, so let the planning begin.

- ♥ Set your date. Give yourself 2-3 months or at least 30 days of planning when you choose a date for your wedding.

- ♥ Consider a day and date when family and friends in and out of your city may attend.

- ♥ Consider the availability of the location for your wedding and reception.

- ♥ Purchase:
    - ♥ A journal
    - ♥ A pocketed three ring binder with 12-15 lines pages for starter
    - ♥ Glue
    - ♥ Or use a shoe box. Use it to organize the planning details, from budget spreadsheets to invitation samples

- ♥ Apply for your marriage license. Keep in mind that some states require an application and blood test 30 days prior to your wedding date.

- ♥ Contracts are necessary. To ensure your wedding day will flow smoothly and you will have the details you have requested for the wedding of your dream, be sure you get it in writing. It is very important to read every line of the contract before signing it. Make a list of the important details you would like to see and incorporate them in the contracts as necessary. If you do not understand a line-item in the contract, ask for clarity.

- ♥ Stand firm when working with suppliers. When you are not sure, stay calm and don't make a hasty decision. This could be an expensive lesson. Instead, take the time to think about it and go back to the supplier if necessary.

♥ Seek wise counsel. Premarital counseling will help you connect more deeply with your future spouse. You need to effectively talk. Communication is enhanced through counseling and more than likely you will see areas that may need attention for building a healthy foundation in your marriage.

♥ Be truthful. Keep in mind your main focus during the planning of your wedding is on having a **BIG MARRIAGE**.

♥ Brace yourself. Your wedding day will come swiftly. It is important to do something every day. However, the time you put into a beautiful wedding will never compare to the promise of forever, nor the time, intensity and focus needed after you say 'I Do'.

♥ Know what you love, what is important to you and what you can live without.

♥ Stay cool and do not allow yourself to become overwhelmed with the planning of your wedding.

♥ Have fun and laugh a lot.

♥ Take Notes

Marriage License Information

In order to hold a wedding ceremony, you must first have a marriage license. There are many requirements regarding marriage licenses that differ from state-to-state. The list below highlights a few common requirements for obtaining your marriage licenses.

- ༪ Begin by calling or emailing your County Clerk's Office with specific questions. Such as,
    - o How soon should we apply for our marriage license?
    - o How long is our marriage license valid?
    - o What is the fee for the marriage license?
    - o Is a blood test required?
- ༪ A wedding date must be set prior to applying for a license. In most counties, the license is effective for a limited time.
    - o The bride and groom must apply for the license together.
    - o Each person must bring in a certified copy of his or her birth certificate.
    - o Social Security Cards.
    - o You may need proof of residency.
    - o If you are under age 18, a parent must accompany you to give consent.
- ༪ There is a marriage fee, payable at the time of filing an application.
- ༪ If you have been married before, you must provide proof of a divorce or annulment. Some counties require a waiting period before remarrying.

Notes for Getting Started

_____

_____

_____

_____

_____

_____

_____

_____

_____

_____

_____

_____

_____

_____

_____

_____

_____

_____

_____

_____

_____

_____

_____

_____

_____

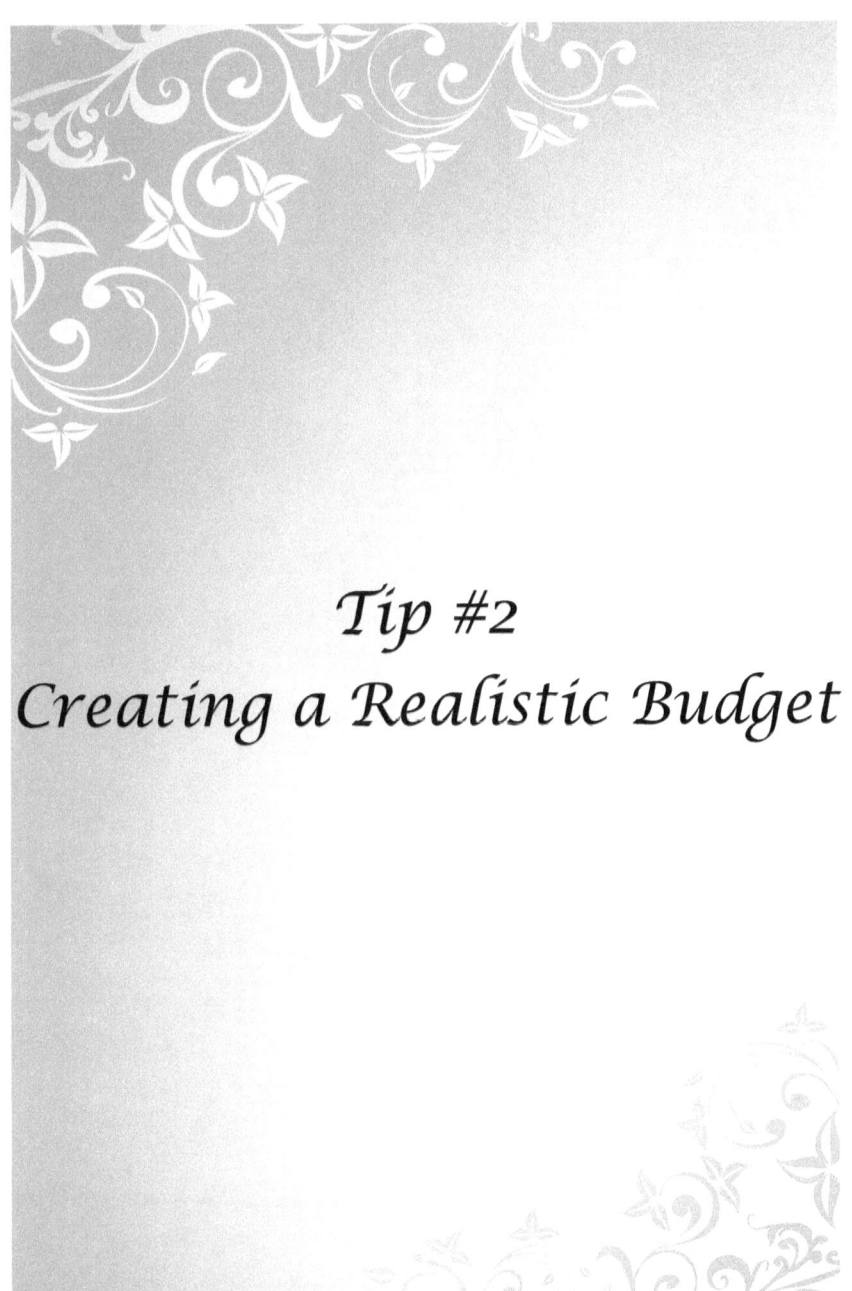

Tip #2
Creating a Realistic Budget

Tip #2   Creating a Realistic Budget

- ♥ You have little time, so the more detailed in your thinking you are about what should be included in your wedding the better.

- ♥ Prioritize items of importance
    - ♥ A gown or a suit
    - ♥ A day wedding or evening wedding
    - ♥ A weekday or weekend

- ♥ Would you prefer
    - ♥ A sit-down dinner
    - ♥ An hors d'oeuvres reception
    - ♥ A buffet reception
    - ♥ A cake-and-punch reception

- ♥ Consider for your budget
    - ♥ Printed invitations
    - ♥ Electronic invitations
    - ♥ Or word-of-mouth method to invite your guests to the ceremony and reception

- ♥ Whenever possible, use cash. You will avoid overspending and accumulating credit card debt. If you are not paying off your credit card balance at the end of the month, your wedding expenses will incur compounding interest. This means you are now spending more for your wedding than budgeted. Creating debt should be avoided at all cost. Financial problems are one of the leading ongoing problems for couples.

- ♥ Be very careful not to get involved in emotional spending. Inexpensive items can be beautiful and expensive items do not mean they are best suited for your wedding day. Your wedding can and will be beautiful within budget.

♥ Be Friendly and flexible. If you need to spend more on a particular item than budgeted, look for ways to cut back on other items to stay within your budget.

♥ Will you use decorations and flowers at the ceremony and at the reception?

♥ Research bridal magazines. Use the library as a resource. Ready reference at the library is free and an excellent resource for locating information and hard to find information.

♥ Browse new and used bookstores. This research will provide pictures and ideas for planning and communicating your thoughts and dreams of your wedding day to your wedding coordinator and other individuals involved.

♥ Ask recent brides for helpful books they may be willing to share.

♥ Your budget checklist is on page 85.

♥ Take Notes

Did you know?

Two money saving tips:

1. A weekday wedding can be substantially less and more economical than a weekend wedding, depending on the space and location.

2. Search the Internet. You can find various wedding-related web sites, some offering free e-mail invitations, helpful articles, vendors and useful worksheets.

Notes for Creating a Realistic Budget

Tip #3
Secure a Location

Tip #3   Securing a Location

♥ Consider what you love. Will your budget agree with your dream location? Keep an open mind. Some locations do not need decorations. The beauty may be provided and the ambiance set. Visit places you are considering.

♥ Are you an outdoors person? Give thought to hold your nuptial ceremony near your favorite place of peace and tranquility. Locations may include a park, at a lakefront or near the ocean.

♥ Traditional wedding settings include:
  - ♥ Churches
  - ♥ Chapels
  - ♥ Cathedrals
  - ♥ Synagogues
  - ♥ Temples
  - ♥ Or other places of worship

♥ Other ceremony sites are:
  - ♥ Beaches
  - ♥ Beautiful room
  - ♥ Clubs
  - ♥ Flower garden
  - ♥ Halls
  - ♥ Hotels
  - ♥ Home of a friend
  - ♥ Your home
  - ♥ Museum
  - ♥ Parks

♥ Ask about square footage at each site before you fall in love with it. A rule of thumb for the ceremony is to allot 10 square feet per person. For a dinner-and-dancing reception, aim for 20 square feet per person. These numbers will guarantee ample elbow room for your guests.

♥ Remember, it is not how much money you spend, but how you spend your money.

♥ Take Notes

Notes for Securing Your Location

Tip #4
Notify An Officiant

Tip #4 Notify An Officiant

♥ You are not limited to a Pastor, Priest, or Rabbi. Any individual holding clergy certified credentials is qualified to perform your ceremony. For non-religious weddings, he or she might be a justice of the peace, Magistrate or even the Captain of a ship (when onboard).

♥ An Officiant is someone who officiates (leads) a service or ceremony, such as a marriage ceremony. Respectfully interview potential Officiant to ensure that all of your questions are comfortably answered. Also ask the Officiant if they provide premarital counseling sessions. Premarital counseling increases your ability to have a 'Big Marriage'. A big marriage' focus is on a solid and lifelong marriage.

♥ Will the Officiant be available during the times you need him or her? An hour is usually considered appropriate.

♥ Consider utilizing only one hour of their time for the ceremony. Plan your rehearsal mindful of the one hour block of time if he or she is able to come.

♥ What are the fees? If applicable, most officiants appreciate receiving their fees prior to the ceremony. Unless otherwise specified, one day prior is acceptable. The groom may also put this fee in a sealed envelope and give it to his best man or wedding consultant who gives it to the officiant either before or immediately after the ceremony. The fee may range from $50 to $300.

♥ Some officiants may not accept a fee, depending on your relationship with the bride and groom. If the officiant's fee is refused, send a donation to their church or synagogue.

Notes for Notifying An Officiant

_____

_____

_____

_____

_____

_____

_____

_____

_____

_____

_____

_____

_____

_____

_____

_____

_____

_____

_____

_____

_____

_____

_____

_____

Tip #5
Creating a Guest List

Tip #5   Creating Your Guest List

- ♥ It is important to notify your guests of your wedding date as soon as possible.

- ♥ Decide who you would like to attend and how many guests you would like in all.

- ♥ Create your guest list in a timely manner.

- ♥ Develop your list with your fiancé, close family members and friends.

- ♥ If your guest list is too large for your budget, try to compromise.
  - ♥ A large wedding with a small reception.
  - ♥ A large wedding and a dancing party.
  - ♥ A large wedding and a picnic reception.
  - ♥ A large wedding with a cake and punch reception.
  - ♥ A large wedding with no reception.
  - ♥ A large engagement party with an intimate wedding.
  - ♥ A large engagement party and then elope.

- ♥ Are your guests coming from out of town? Overnight accommodations should be made for them. You are not obligated to pay for their hotel stay or travel arrangements, but offer them leads on hotels and other travel-related details.

- ♥ **Sending invitations**. Your wedding invitation is the first visual statement your guests will see of you and your fiancé as you begin your new life together. Send out invitations that are a reflection of your style and the formality of the wedding. Before ordering, proofread the location, date, time, spelling, wording, etc.

- ♥ If time permits,

- ♥ Order invitations four to six months before the wedding.
- ♥ Send out your invitations six to eight weeks before the wedding.

♥ If time and money is limited,

- ♥ Invite your guests by calling them on the telephone
- ♥ Invite your guests using email
- ♥ Invite your guests with a handwritten note
- ♥ Purchase your invitations at a stationary or card store. Do not use oversized envelopes. Additional postage is required.

♥ Inviting your guests via e-mail is an informal approach; however, electronic invitations are becoming more popular for casual and informal weddings and weddings with limited budgets.

♥ The response cards are designed to ask your invited guests to Rsvp, an abbreviation for the French words 'répondez s'il vous plait'. Répondez s'il vous plait means, please reply. When a reply is requested via telephone or electronic mail and your response window is less than 30 days or when asking your guests to send back the reply card, follow up may be required.

- ♥ Unfortunately, 20-25% of your invited guests will not formally reply or attend. Ask a close friend or family member to take on the task of following up with your guests.
- ♥ Maintain an accurate guest list with their names, complete addresses, and telephone numbers.

♥ The craft oriented bride and groom may create and design their invitations. Items for the invitations can be purchased at an arts and crafts store. Another idea is to purchase wedding oriented card stock paper from office supply stores and print your wedding information from your personal computer.

♥ Discuss if children are invited to the wedding and if they are invited to the reception. It is your choice. If you decide not to include children, it is appropriate to say, "An Adult Affair" or "Please, Adults Only" on your invitations or response cards.

♥ Do not include registry information or your cash only preference on your wedding invitation or in the same envelope as your wedding invitations. It is in poor taste and too much like asking for gifts. You may have cash needs; however your guests are invited for the purpose of celebrating your marriage, not to bring gifts. Tell your closest friends or family members that cash gifts are welcome and allow word-of-mouth to work for you.

♥ Take Notes

Did you know?

When you address the envelope, it should include the guests intended to come to the ceremony and reception. Your Rsvp list will correspond to the guests you have invited to the ceremony, reception, bridal shower and bachelor party.

For example, if your envelope is addressed to Mr. and Mrs. Jones, you are only expecting Mr. and Mrs. Jones. Another example is Ms. Smith and Guest. In this case, Ms. Smith is invited to bring one person. When you address the envelope to Ms. Sara Smith, Ms. Smith is not invited to bring a guest. The expectation is she will come alone.

Notes for Creating Your Guest List

_____
_____
_____
_____
_____
_____
_____
_____
_____
_____
_____
_____
_____
_____
_____
_____
_____
_____
_____
_____
_____
_____
_____
_____
_____
_____

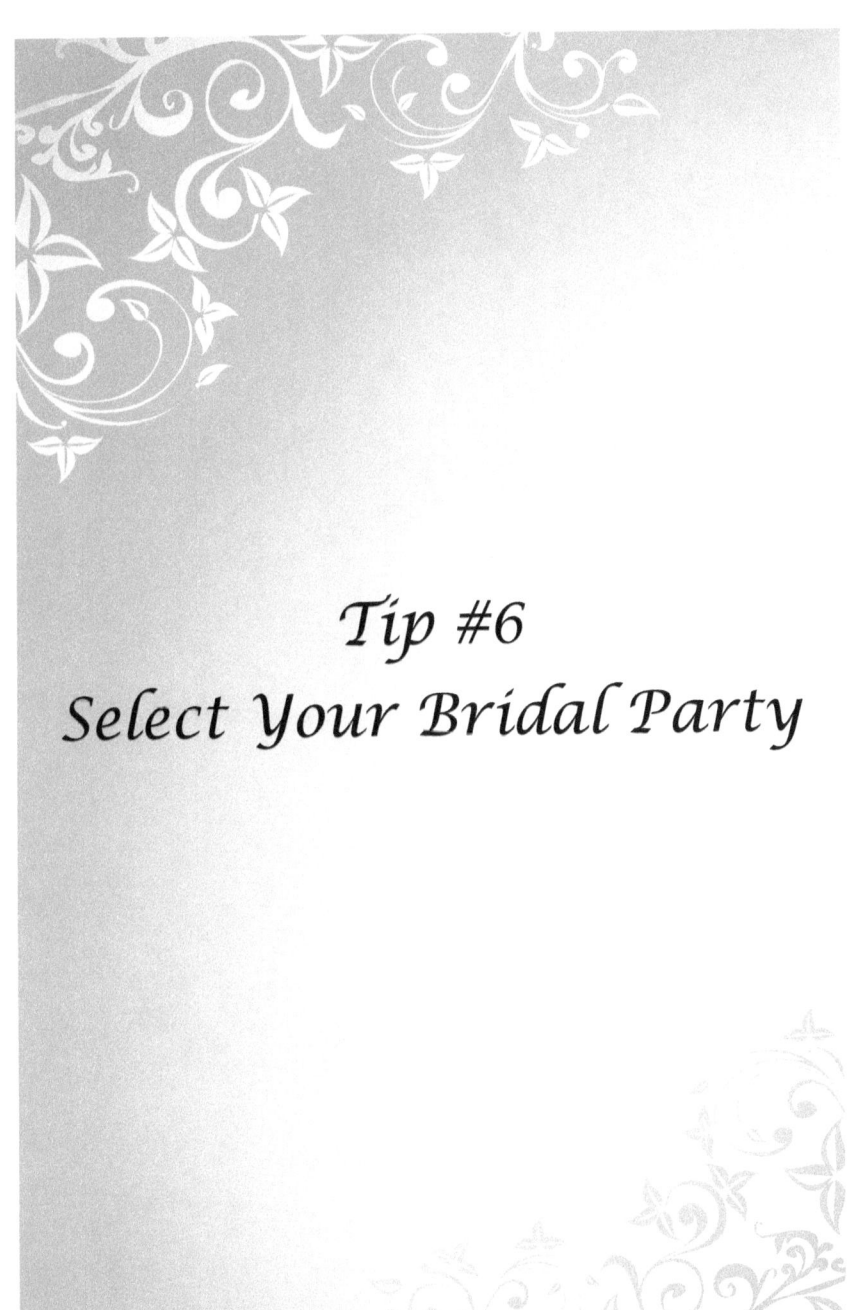

Tip #6
Select Your Bridal Party

Tip #6 Selecting Your Bridal Party

- ♥ The bridal party includes:
    - ♥ A Bridesmaids,
    - ♥ A Matron of Honor,
    - ♥ A Maid of Honor,
    - ♥ The Best Man and
    - ♥ Groomsmen.

- ♥ The maid of honor is customarily an unmarried female, while the matron of honor is a married female.

- ♥ Consider one bridesmaid and groomsmen for every 50 guests. Typically, no more than six bridesmaids and groomsmen (although we know some brides exceed that number).

- ♥ Narrow your choices based on bridesmaids that are close to you and four personality traits:
    - ♥ Dependability
    - ♥ Stability
    - ♥ Availability
    - ♥ Trust to support you and fiancé

- ♥ Your bridesmaid should have the ability to pay for expenses. Inform them of the expected commitment before they commit.

- ♥ Your invitation to the bridesmaid is permanent. Think carefully about the person you want standing on your side. There are other positions to fill: your vocalist and ushers, poem or scripture reader, manning the gift table, etc.

- ♥ Be mindful of the anticipated expenses for your bridal party. Your wedding experience should be pleasurable for everyone.

- **Their Attire**. Consider what you want the bridesmaid to wear and what color it should be. Remember that attire includes shoes, jewelry and undergarments.

- Bridesmaid dresses may complement each other. Uniqueness of individual gowns allows each woman to shine. Complementing gowns versus matching gowns is helpful when the bridesmaids shape and dress sizes are different. For continuity's sake, your color scheme should be kept simple and the fabrics similar.

- If your preference is for your bridesmaids to wear the same dress, add sleeves or a wrap to flatter all sizes.

- There is no need for all the women in your bridal party to wear identical necklaces, shoes and headpieces.

- The old saying, "Less is best" often remains true. Your wedding can be elegant, fashionable and strikingly tasteful. Based on this adage, create a balance between your bridesmaids' outfits not being too bare or overly accessorized.

- Visual how you want their hair and makeup? Write it down.

- Does anyone in your bridal party have to travel? Will they stay with family, friends, or in a hotel? Although not necessary, it is a wonderful gesture for you to pay for their accommodations. Either way, communicate upfront the expenses you are willing to pay.

- Remember to budget for small, thoughtful gifts of appreciation for the wedding party. Be creative. Such tokens might include necklaces, earrings, cuff links, neck-ties, complimentary spa treatments, and store gift cards. The choices are endless. Have fun, and release any nervous tension. It is the thought that counts.

- Take Notes

Notes for Selecting Your Bridal Party

The next few tips include the brides' attire, flowers, your rings, photography and the food. These tips can be big-ticket items. Keep in mind what you love. Know what is important to you and what you can live without. Most of all stay focused. Stay focused on your fiancé, your budget and the big picture.

These items will pull on your heartstring. **DO NOT** sway from your budget and remember to use cash as often as possible. Each time you use cash to purchase your necessities you are empowering your marriage and giving yourself a good start. An abundance of debt has great potential to shake a solid foundation. Limited debt empowers your marriage and creates a solid foundation.

Accept help when possible and remember a **BIG MARRIAGE, a solid foundation, and longevity** are your ultimate goals!

Tip #7
The Brides Attire

Something old
Something new
Something borrowed
Something blue

By Anonymous

Something Old, Something New, Something
Borrowed, Something Blue
And a sixpence in your shoe

Something old refers to wearing an item that represents a connection with the bride's family and her old life. Usually, the bride wears a piece of family jewelry or maybe her mother or grandmother's wedding dress.

Wearing **something new** represents good fortune and success in the bride's new life. The bride's dress, if new, can be considered for this or any other new piece she'll wear.

Wearing **something borrowed** from a happy bride at her wedding is meant to bring good fortune to the marriage. Something borrowed is usually an item of bridal clothing, a piece of jewelry or a handkerchief.

Something blue dates back to biblical times when the color blue represented purity and loyalty. Over the years this has evolved from wearing blue clothing to wearing a blue garter band on one or both thighs.

Tip #7   The Bride's Attire

♥   By now you should have decided on the date, time and location of the ceremony. Most women have tucked away in a corner of their mind a vision of how she would like to be dressed on her wedding day.

♥   Are you wearing a gown, evening dress or suit? You can use this day to experiment with fashion and reinvent your style. Consider your purchasing options.

  ♥   Will you buy new or secondhand

  ♥   Will you borrow or rent

  If you feel as though your budget will restrict your options, don't be discouraged. Having a set budget does not mean you cannot get the look you want. You can still "WOW" your guests. Rely on your sense of what looks best on you and what will make you feel extra special, comfortable, and confident.

♥   Bridal magazines are a great resource. Look through the magazines to find the look you like. Cut out the dress that will look best on your body type and maximize your assets, even if it is out of your price range. Take the picture to the clerk at the bridal store and find a dress that is similar within your price range. If you are getting married within 30 days you may have to purchase a dress or suit off the rack or pay for a rush on an ordered gown and allow time for alterations.

♥   Buyer beware –

  ♥   Gowns often fail to arrive on time

  ♥   Most gowns require a larger size

  ♥   Check the reputation of the bridal boutique

  ♥   Seek an independent tailor that specializes in bridal gown alterations

  ♥   Ask the tailor for pricing and time needed for completion in advance

- ♥ There are a few basic guidelines:
  - ♥ The more formal the wedding, the more luxurious the gown. Customarily, floor length, full-skirted gowns with a cathedral, chapel or sweep train. The bride carries a cascading to medium size bouquet.
  - ♥ For a semi-formal wedding, the gown is floor-length with a chapel train and small bouquet.
  - ♥ The bride who has an informal wedding usually wears a street length gown, dress or a suit and a corsage or small bouquet.

- ♥ What the bride wears sets the tone and determines what the groom will wear. Typically, all eyes are on the bride. The bride is always the most beautiful woman at the wedding. The attendants, as well as the groom should complement the bride, never overshadow her.

- ♥ **Your Accessories** - Do not overlook the fine details, such as, your earrings, a necklace, a veil, a hat, a headpiece, gloves and shoes.
  - ♥ Your fabric shoes can be easily embellished. Simply use a glue gun to apply the matching lace or beading for a one-of-a-kind accessory.
  - ♥ Consider the best height for comfort and for standing next to your groom.
  - ♥ Break in your shoes to make sure you are comfortable on your wedding day.

- ♥ Some boutiques offer a free headpiece or veil with the purchase of a gown. Make sure you ask for this before purchasing your gown.
  - ♥ Very Formal Wedding – Full-length veil and elaborate headpiece
  - ♥ Formal daytime wedding – Fingertip veil or hat
  - ♥ Formal evening wedding – Beyond fingertip veil

- ♥ Semiformal wedding – Fingertip veil
- ♥ Informal wedding – No veil

♥ **Flawless Skin, Beautiful Hair and Healthy Nails** begin months before you say 'I do' and from the inside out.

♥ **Your Make-up.** Beautiful make-up begins with flawless skin. Drink lots of water, eat fresh fruit and vegetables, rest your body, and laugh; it is good like medicine.

♥ The most important part of your wedding day make-up is to look yourself, not made-up. The day may be long and countless photographs are taken. Make-up will help you look radiant through it all. The best way to ensure this is to practice, practice, and practice. Go to make-up counters and get ideas. Many make-up companies offer complimentary make-overs by their make-up artists. The makeup companies are making it convenient for you to know how the product will look on and they have great expectations for you to make a purchase.

♥ Consider a make-up artist, if you will not apply your own make-up. The make-up artist can help you achieve a natural, but glamorous appearance that will look great in person and in your photographs. You can either go to the salon or have the make-up artist come to your home or wedding dressing site. Negotiate having your make-up free of charge or at a discount in exchange for bringing your mother, your fiancé's mother and your bridal party to receive services.

♥ **Your Hair.** Beautiful hair begins with daily maintenance. Consult with a hairstylist for an at home daily regimen and make your appointment for your day of hair styling. If you are wearing a veil, make your consultation appointment with your veil to ensure having the look you desire with no disappointments or surprises the day of your wedding. Negotiate having your hair styled free of charge or at a discount in exchange for bringing your mother, fiancé's mother and your bridal party to the salon.

♥ **Your Nails**. Healthy Nails. Your wedding day will be filled with handshakes and people admiring your ring. Plan to treat yourself to a relaxing manicure and pedicure. Manicures are care for your hands and pedicures are care for your feet. Pedicures enhance your feet appearance, especially when wearing open-toed shoes. Manicures and pedicures are great tension relievers for the bride and groom. If you cannot pay full price for these services, do your own manicure and pedicure or negotiate having your nails serviced free of charge or at a discount in exchange for bringing your mother, your fiancé's mother and your bridal party to the nail spa.

♥ Bridal Attire Checklist
- ♥ Full slip
- ♥ Garter
- ♥ Gloves
- ♥ Gown
- ♥ Handbag
- ♥ Hairdresser
- ♥ Headpiece
- ♥ Jewelry
- ♥ Lingerie
- ♥ Make-up Artist
- ♥ Manicure/Pedicure
- ♥ Panty hose
- ♥ Petticoat or slip
- ♥ Shoes
- ♥ Something Old
- ♥ Something New
- ♥ Something Borrowed
- ♥ Something Blue
- ♥ Veil/Hat

Notes for The Brides Attire

_____

_____

_____

_____

_____

_____

_____

_____

_____

_____

_____

_____

_____

_____

_____

_____

_____

_____

_____

_____

_____

_____

_____

_____

_____

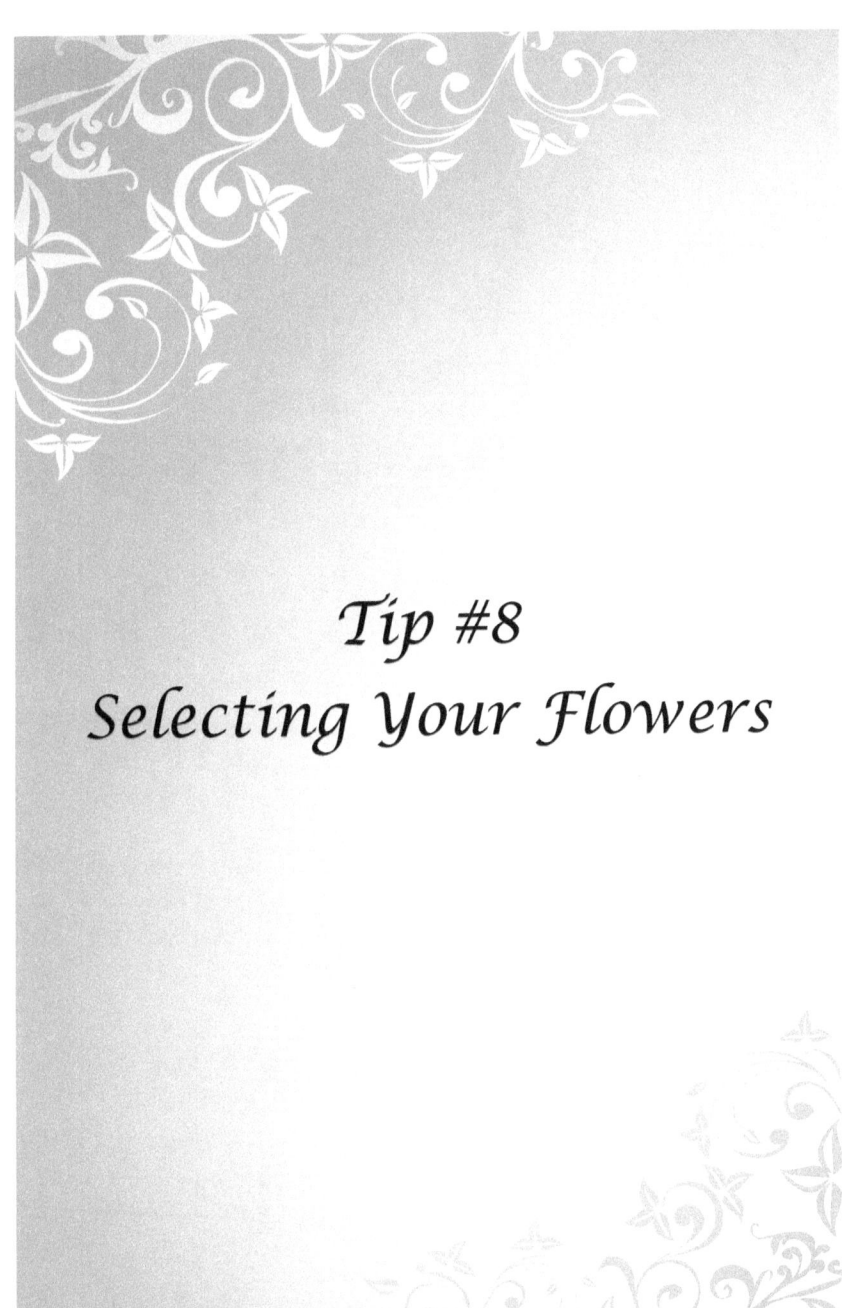

Tip #8
Selecting Your Flowers

Tip #8   Selecting Your Flowers

During Victorian times, flowers took on an additional significance, as lovers would send messages to each other using different flowers, with each flower having its own meaning. These associations were soon the assumed way of designing the bride's bouquet and are still used today by many brides.

♥ Consider fresh flowers for a fantastic and elegant appearance. Have an idea of what you want and know the mood you want to create.

♥ Be daring!

♥ Think of your favorite flowers. Look through magazines and cut out pictures as references.

♥ A good solution is to combine three seasonal flowers in a round burst of blossoms which are either hand-tied or packed into a bouquet holder. Choosing seasonal flowers gives you a plentiful selection. For example, in June roses are in variety and color and in October mums are available in beautiful fall colors.

♥ Ask a talented friend or family member to assist with decorating the bouquets and corsages.

♥ Don't hesitate to visit a pricy floral designer. A real professional can help you focus on what is important and often will rise to the challenge of working with limited funds.

♥ The bride's bouquet is an essential accessory to her wedding ensemble. It can be as much a focal point as your wedding gown. However, carrying a bouquet is completely up to you. Other options might be:

   ♥ To carry a beautiful flower ball

   ♥ A selection of long stemmed flowers

   ♥ A mixture of blossoms and greenery that fall into an elongated, trailing shape

   ♥ The winter bride might opt for beautifully decorated hand muffs.

- ♥ The bride may also opt to carry nothing at all. Be creative as your options are many.

- ♥ **Additional Flower Checklist.**
  - ♥ Bouquets:
    - ☐ Bride, Bridesmaids and Jr. Bridesmaid
  - ♥ Flower girl's rose petals
  - ♥ Corsages:
    - ☐ Mothers and Grandmothers
    - ☐ Godmother and hostesses receive smaller corsages
  - ♥ Boutonnieres:
    - ☐ Groom, Groomsmen, Ushers, Fathers, Grandfathers, Ring bearer and Godfather
  - ♥ Aisle decorations, if applicable
  - ♥ Altar arrangements, if applicable
  - ♥ Pew decorations, if applicable
  - ♥ The cake table traditionally has the bride's bouquet placed on it during the reception.
  - ♥ A bouquet to toss, if applicable
- ♥ Take Notes

Did You Know?

Brides can share the cost of decorations. This will provide both weddings with more than one bride can afford on her own. With this scenario, silk flowers may provide the best choice to avoid wilting. Check to see if another wedding is scheduled to take place where your wedding will take place. Or, if there is a bride you trust that is getting married close to your date willing to share flowers and decorations.

Optimal, effective communication and maybe a contract is needed to take advantage of shared flowers and decorations, but it can be done.

Notes for Selecting Your Flowers

Tip #9
Your Rings

Tip #9   Your Rings

♥ When a bride offers her left hand to her groom it is the beginning of their married life together. Your rings symbolize continuous faithfulness and unending love.

♥ Before you shop, review your budget and establish an amount for your rings. This amount should not compromise your overall wedding budget. There are many rings you will see and love, so look for those priced within your budget. Remember that pawn and consignment shops also carry beautiful, inexpensive jewelry.

♥ Shop around for a jeweler that accepts trade-in jewelry, so that you can trade-up. Trading-up lowers the original purchase price.

   ♥ Your trade-in jewelry, for example may be a gold or platinum necklaces, rings, and bracelets that are not important to you. This is the jewelry you have forgotten about and you do not mind parting with or that you are willing to part with. Think carefully about trading-in jewelry that still holds sentimental value.

♥ Keep in mind what you love. As early as the 15th century diamonds delighted well-to-do brides. "Hard" stones like diamonds, rubies and sapphires can be worn daily over an extended period of time without much damage. "Soft" stones like emeralds, opals and pearls are also popular, but they are more likely to scratch, crack or chip if worn daily.

♥ Do you love

   ♥ Rings with a single stone

   ♥ Rings with a cluster of stones or

   ♥ Do you love bands with or without stones?

♥ Also consider if you want your stone set in yellow gold, white gold, platinum, or even titanium. There are many options. You will "fall in love" repeatedly and more than likely come back to your first ring of choice. Do not stress about it. You will know when you have located the ring of your dreams within your budget. There is always the option to begin your 'Big Marriage' with his and hers wedding bands. They are classic and very reasonable.

♥ If your fiancé chooses to surprise you, please discuss your preference ahead of time. Your communication should clarify your desires and eliminate any potential disappointment.

♥ When budgeting for your fiancé's ring, discuss his likes and dislikes.

♥ A sweet reminder of your commitment and unfailing love for each other is to inscribe a message in the inside of the ring.

♥ Take Notes

Did you know?

The bride's engagement ring and wedding ring are traditionally worn on the third finger of the left hand (the finger next to your little finger). There is no specific evidence to explain the onset of this tradition; however, as Egyptian legend suggests that the ring finger follows the vena amoris, that is, the vein of love that runs directly to the heart.

Notes for Your Rings

_____

_____

_____

_____

_____

_____

_____

_____

_____

_____

_____

_____

_____

_____

_____

_____

_____

_____

_____

_____

_____

_____

Tip #10
Capturing Your Day

Tip #10   Capturing Your Day

♥ Photographs and wedding videos are very important keepsakes. Long after the wedding ceremony photographs remain. Whether taken by friends or a professional, every photo becomes more precious with time. Each photo will capture memories that will last a lifetime.

♥ **The Photographer.** When hiring a photographer be sure they specialize in weddings. Be sure to stay within your established budget and check references. Ask your photographer to use your proofs as part of your album package to save developing costs.

♥ Communicate with the photographer your desire for a mixture of different poses and pictures. In fact, days before the wedding, offer the photographer a list of all images you want to be sure to get. Your wedding day goes quickly, and you will long to see it captured forever.

♥ Another idea is to ask your guests to take candid snapshots using their digital cameras and/or disposable cameras that you provide at the ceremony and reception. This offers an alternative to a professional photographer.

♥ Videography is the next best way to preserve your wedding memories. The mood of your wedding day will be captured in motion and sound. Memories you may remember, such as the vows, the kisses, laughter and excitement and other possible bloopers, sentiments of your guests and tears of joy you may not have known occurred.

♥ **The Videographer.** Be sure you hire a videographer that specializes in weddings and ask to see samples of his or her work.

  ♥ **Documentary** style of production records your wedding day as it happens in real time. Very little editing is involved. This preference is less expensive and can be delivered within days after the wedding. Another production style is more **theatrical**. This includes more editing, two or more cameras, studio time, and is more expensive.

♥ Days before the wedding, offer the videographer that is shooting your wedding a list of all images you want captured at the wedding and reception.

♥ Consider hiring a company that offers both videography and photography. Negotiate a savings by combining the two services.

♥ If you are not within budget, ask the price to video tape the ceremony or reception only.

♥ Another option is to ask a friend or family member to videotape your wedding. This is a very high-pressure job. So clearly state your request and list of all images you want captured. Communication is key.

♥ Ask if there is a fee for extra copies of the final production. If it is acceptable with your videographer, get permission to burn DVD's on your computer.

♥ Take Notes

Notes for Capturing Your Day

Tip #11
Your Delectable Edibles

Tip #11 Your Delectable Edibles

♥ Does your budget allow for a reception? If so, secure your location. A deposit equal to about 50 percent of your total cost may be required.

♥ Refer to your invitation list when deciding how large your space needs to be.

♥ Fortunately, many caterers have shared a golden nugget that is an unfortunate truth. Approximately 25 percent of those who agree to attend your reception may not. Remember this formula when ordering meals and your cake. Be careful. This can be tricky. Most chefs and caterers always prepare a few extras but you are only charged for what you order. Ask for details.

♥ Your reception should include comfort foods. These are foods your guests are sure to enjoy.

♥ Consider a cake-and-punch reception with elegant music in the background as an alternative to a sit-down meal or buffet.

♥ **Your Wedding cakes** can be as simple or as elaborate as your wedding. The cake is often the focus of reception decorations and the food. There are cheesecakes, fruit-filled cakes, classic butter cakes, and chocolate cakes. You can get your cake decorated with jewels, hand-painted flowers, fresh flowers, and with chocolate shaped like flowers. If your mind can imagine it, a baker can probably create your dream cake. It is a rare bride who knows exactly what type of cake to choose. Picture in your mind the cake you want and make a sketch.

♥ Another consideration is to provide the pastry chef with a photograph of a cake you want to replicate.

♥ Also ask to see the baker's portfolio of photographs. Your cake is likely to be at the center of attention at the reception.

♥ The price range for wedding cakes is broad. Ask for referrals and set up times with the baker to sample cake choices.

  ♥ Your local grocery stores may be a great place to find cakes for a reasonable price. If you choose to purchase your cake from the grocery store, be sure to assign someone to pick it up at the appointed time. Or,

  ♥ Purchase a small decorated layer cake and serve decorated sheet cakes.

  ♥ Tiers of cupcakes are becoming more popular and non-traditional modern brides are following this trend.

♥ Time seems to pause when the bride and groom settle down to cut the cake. You will want a cake that you both love.

♥ Savor the moment. *Enjoy!*

  ♥ If you get a cake from a bakery, the bakery will have someone deliver it. Make sure that someone will be available to receive the cake in time for your reception. To eliminate having to move your cake after it has been delivered, have your cake table decorated at the designated arrival time. And, remember that your overall reception costs may include a cake-slicing fee.

♥ Alcohol, like champagne and wines will drive up your bottom line. Consider what is important to make your day fantastic. Also, note that most establishments have a corking fee, meaning you will have to pay for the bottles that are opened for you. Ask your reception hall contact person for details.

♥ If your budget does not allow for a reception right away, you may choose what is often called, "Delayed Gratification", a post-wedding gathering for friends and family to celebrate your nuptials. This type of reception can be hosted within a year of the wedding.

♥ Take Notes

Notes for Your Delectable Edibles

Tip #12
The Arts

Tip # 12   The Arts

♥ Most traditional wedding will have musicians, singers, and other artists to perform during the ceremony. You may also have a dancer(s), prayer and someone to read poetry and the scriptures.

♥ Will you need a piano for the pianist or a keyboard? Or, will a CD or iPod provide the music? String or wind instrument solos make for an elegant and wonderful way to create a romantic ambiance.

♥ You will need one usher per 50 guests.

♥ Here is a traditional wedding program outline:

   ♥ Prelude (Instrumental music 15 minutes before the start of the wedding)

   ♥ Lighting of Candles (At the start time, usually by the ushers)

   ♥ A Song, Poem, Prayer or Dance

   ♥ Entrance of Grandparents (First the Groom's, then the Bride's) usually accompanied by soft music

   ♥ Entrance of Parents (First the Groom's, then the Bride's) usually accompanied by soft music

   ♥ A Song, Poem, or Dance

   ♥ Entrance of Officiant, Groom and Best Man

   ♥ Entrance of Bridesmaids and Groomsmen

      □ *Maid of Honor*

      □ *Matron of Honor*

      □ *Ring Bearer*

      □ *Flower Girl*

- ♥ Entrance of Bride (Father or another strong male figure like a brother or uncle walks bride to meet the Groom) Audience is usually directed to stand

- ♥ Officiant begins the Pronouncement

- ♥ Introduction of Married Couple

- ♥ Exit to form Receiving Line (With the married couple leaving first and then the rest of the party following behind)

- ♥ Receiving lines, once an essential wedding tradition, have been losing popularity in recent years. Some couples view them as time-consuming and choose not to incorporate them into their weddings. Etiquette does require, however, for the bride and groom to make an attempt to greet and thank each guest for sharing in their special day. If you decide to incorporate a receiving line, you do not have to include the entire bridal party. Nowadays, most are made up of the bride, groom, and their parents.

- ♥ Take Notes

Did you know?

During the marriage ceremony, the bride stands on the left and the groom on the right. The origin of this, based on ancient folklore, dates back years ago when a groom would capture his bride by kidnapping her. If the groom had to fight off the other men who also wanted her as their bride, he would hold his bride-to-be with his left hand, allowing his right to be free to use his sword.

Notes for The Arts

Tip #13
Rehearse Your Day

Tip #13   Rehearse Your Day

♥   This is the time to get a mental snapshot of your day and work through the details. Begin with the lighting of the candles and work your way through the entire proposed program.

♥   Usually, everyone is in attendance for the rehearsal with the exception of the Officiant unless he/she would prefer to be present. Be sure to negotiate this time with your musicians, dancers, and singers.

♥   Time is of the essence. Give yourself 1 to 1.5 hours to complete the rehearsal. This time frame is possible if you have your details worked out and your wedding coordinator has a clear picture of what you want your wedding day to look like. Remember, the more informed your coordinator is, the smoother your wedding day will probably go.

♥   After the rehearsal, it is appropriate, if budgeted, to host a rehearsal dinner. This can be held at the rehearsal site, a special home, or at a nearby restaurant. It should be a light-hearted time to mingle and meet family and friends.

♥   Traditionally, the groom's family is responsible for the cost of this occasion. However, the majority of couples today pay for the cost of their wedding and all the trimmings.

♥   Take Notes

Notes for Rehearse Your Day

Tip #14
Delegation Is Key

Tip #14   Delegation is Key

- ♥ Please consider the amount of work planning a wedding can be and secure adequate help. You will need to delegate or divide duties to adequately prepare for your wedding-especially if it is within 30 days. To help you start your list of areas that you will want to have others assist you include:

  - ♥ Sampling food and cake
  - ♥ Reserving wedding and reception sites
  - ♥ Remembering to pick up and pay for licenses
  - ♥ Hiring musicians and other artists
  - ♥ Picking up men's tuxedo rentals
  - ♥ Picking up bridesmaids gowns and alterations
  - ♥ Selecting flowers
  - ♥ Remembering to bring rings

- ♥ When the bride walks down the aisle, all of the planning should come together. At this point, you are a radiant bride, not a woman with an abundance of details to organize. This is your moment. This is your day to shine.

- ♥ Ask someone skilled you trust to be the wedding coordinator of your dream day.   The coordinator's responsibility is ensuring that everything behind the scenes runs smoothly. Keep in mind the trusted coordinator may charge a fee. If the coordinator does not charge a fee, budget a monetary gift of appreciation anyway. If you do not know of a qualified coordinator, seek a free-lance professional wedding planner who works for a fee.

- ♥ Some churches have wedding coordinators that help with onsite details and may have a lower fee than a wedding planner.

- ♥ Now, get ready to roll up your sleeves because time is moving swiftly.

- ♥ Enjoy your day and look forward to a BIG MARRIAGE!

- ♥ Take Notes

Notes for Delegation Is Key

Your Budget

Your Budget

$ _____

Budgeted / Spent

Expenses

Ceremony

- o Ceremony facility
- o Ceremony miscellaneous
- o Officiant/Clergy
- o Wedding Coordinator

Floral & Decorations

- o Bride's bouquet
- o Boutonnieres
- o Bridesmaid bouquets
- o Flowers miscellaneous
- o Ceremony decorations
- o Reception decorations
- o Entrance decorations
- o Table linens
- o Chair covers

Gifts

- o Bridesmaid gifts
- o Attendants' gifts
- o Parents' gifts
- o Miscellaneous

Honeymoon

- o Airfare

o   Hotel

o   Taxi and Tips

Invitations

o   Wedding invitations

o   Reply cards

o   Inserts

o   Maps

o   Thank you cards

Jewelry

o   Her wedding ring and band

o   His wedding band

o   Bride's jewelry

o   Bridesmaid jewelry

Makeup/Beauty

o   Manicure

o   Pedicure

o   Facial

o   Makeup application

o   Makeup purchase

o   Hair styling

Music & Entertainment

o   Ceremony entertainment

o   Band

o   Disc jockey

o   Rehearsal dinner music

Photography

- o Engagement photos
- o Ceremony
- o Reception
- o Reprints/Extra photos

Reception

- o Beverages/Alcohol
- o Cake
- o Favors
- o Food/Catering
- o Reception miscellaneous

Rehearsal Dinner

- o Beverages/Alcohol
- o Meal
- o Room rental

Rentals

- o Candelabras
- o Chairs
- o Chair covers
- o Aisle runners
- o Tables
- o Other rentals

Transportation

- o Guests' Shuttle
- o Limousine
- o Valet Parking
- o Other transportation details

Videographer

o   Your love-story presentation

o   Video/DVD-extra copies

o   Videography

o   Video miscellaneous

Wedding Attire

o   Alterations

o   Bride's accessories

o   Bride's undergarments

o   Bride's shoes

o   Bridal gown

o   Bridal veil

o   Groom's accessories

o   Groom's tuxedo

Notes for Your Budget

_____

_____

_____

_____

_____

_____

_____

_____

_____

_____

_____

_____

_____

_____

_____

_____

_____

_____

_____

_____

_____

_____

_____

Wedding Checklist

Wedding Checklist

Ceremony

_ Decide on location

_ Choose officiant

_ Select rings

_ Pick attendants

Legal issues

_ Secure marriage license

_ Make name change

_ Change legal will

_ Appoint beneficiary

Reception

_ Choose site of reception

_ Hire caterer

_ Complete guest list

_ Select invitations

_ Verify addresses

_ Make place cards

_ Decide on beverages

_ Choose cake

_ Select music

_ Choose photographer

_ Choose videographer

_ Decide on flowers

_ Pick favors

Wedding attire

_ Select wedding gown

_ Choose groom's attire

_ Select attendant's attire

_ Make beauty appointments

Related events

_ Bridal shower

_ Bachelorette party

_ Bachelor party

_ Plan rehearsal dinner

_ Decide on gift registry

_ Purchase gifts for attendants

_ Purchase thank you notes

Honeymoon

_ Select location

_ Choose trousseau

Guest interests

_ Make accommodations

_ Coordinate transportation

_ Make seating assignments

Post Wedding

_ Write out thank you notes